Rodgers & Hammerstein SOLOS for Kids

The King and I

South Pacific

Oklahoma!

Cinderella

The Sound of Music

FLOWER DRUM SONG

MW01097937

ISBN 978-1-4234-8329-8

WILLIAMSON MUSIC®
A RODGERS AND HAMMERSTEIN COMPANY
www.williamsonmusic.com

EXCLUSIVELY DISTRIBUTED BY

HAL•LEONARD®
CORPORATION
7777 W. BLUEMOUND RD. P.O. BOX 13819 MILWAUKEE, WI 53213

Visit Hal Leonard Online at
www.halleonard.com

ALAN'S MUSIC CENTER, INC
8510 La Mesa Blvd.
La Mesa, CA 91942
(619) 466-1938

SELECTED RECORDING ARTISTS

NICOLE BOCCHI recently appeared as Jane Banks in the Broadway production of *Mary Poppins*. She originated the role of Cindy Lou Who in the Broadway production of *Dr. Seuss' How the Grinch Stole Christmas!*. She appeared in the San Francisco production of *White Christmas*.

LEXIE DeBLASIO appeared in the Broadway tour of *Dr. Seuss' How the Grinch Stole Christmas!*. She has appeared in regional productions of *High School Musical* and *The Sound of Music*. She has performed as soloist at the U.S. Open.

MATTHEW GUMLEY is currently in the Broadway cast of *The Addams Family*. He has appeared in the original Broadway productions of *Mary Poppins* (Michael Banks) and as Chip in Disney's *Beauty and the Beast*. He appeared as Jesse in the Off-Broadway production of *Distracted*. On TV, he has been featured on the animated favorites *Dora the Explorer* and *The Wonder Pets*; as well as *The View* and *Law and Order: SVU*. Matthew created the role of Young Bobby Driscoll in Michael Dansicker's new musical, *Shooting Star*.

KATHERINE McNAMARA is currently appearing as Fredrika in the Broadway production of *A Little Night Music*. She has appeared in regional productions of *The Happy Elf*, *Music Man*, and *Annie*. Her many film credits include *Sam Steele and the Junior Detective* and *Matchmaker Mary* (Silver Hills Pictures).

GABRIELLA MALEK has appeared on Broadway in the role of Jemima in *Chitty Chitty Bang Bang*. On tour, she was featured in *Les Misérables*. TV credits include Tasha in *The Backyardigans* and *Blues Room*. Off-Broadway, she played The Young Princess in the York production of *I and Albert*.

LINDSAY MARON appears at *The American Girl Theatre*. She is featured on the recordings *Kidz Bop 9*, *Kidz Bop 10*, *Kidz Bop Gold* and *Barbie Pop*.

LINA SILVER just completed a run in the new musical *Happiness* at Lincoln Center Theatre. She appeared in The Public Theatre production of *A Midsummer's Night Dream*. On tour, she was featured in *101 Dalmatians* (as Patch) and *A Xmas Story*. Her TV appearances include *Heroes* and Macy's Thanksgiving Parade.

Pianist **LAWRENCE YURMAN** most recently served as Musical Director for the Broadway production of *Grey Gardens*. He also conducted the NY productions of *Side Show*, *A Funny Thing Happened on the Way to the Forum*, and *Thoroughly Modern Millie*. He is currently Music Director for Lea Salonga's North America concert tour.

Producer **MICHAEL E. DANSICKER** has served as arranger, MD, and orchestrator on over 100 NY productions (including: *Singin' in the Rain*, *Dance of the Vampires*, and the Tharp/Dylan *The Times They Are A-Changin'*); as well as musical consultant to a dozen hit films (including: *Elf*, *Analyze That*, *Meet the Parents* and *Brain Donors*). He most recently wrote the dance and incidental music for *Little House on the Prairie* (starring Melissa Gilbert) and is writing the songs (with Bill Meade) and scoring *Garfield Live!* (with Book by Garfield's creator Jim Davis). His newest musical *Shooting Star: The Bobby Driscoll Story* is currently in full development for NY production.

CONTENTS

Pianists on the CD: Lawrence Yurman (tracks 3-14, 17-28),
Louise Lerch (tracks 1, 15)
Hank Powell (tracks 2, 16)

For all except tracks 1, 2, 15, 16:
Recordings engineered at P.P.I. Studios, New York City
Tracks Engineered by Chip Fabrizzi
Piano and Vocal Tracks produced by Michael Dansicker
Special Thanks to: Nancy Carson at Carson Adler Agency, Dale Fabrizzi,
and the Amelia DeMayo Vocal Studios

DITES-MOI
(Tell Me Why)
from *South Pacific*

Lyrics by Oscar Hammerstein II
Music by Richard Rodgers

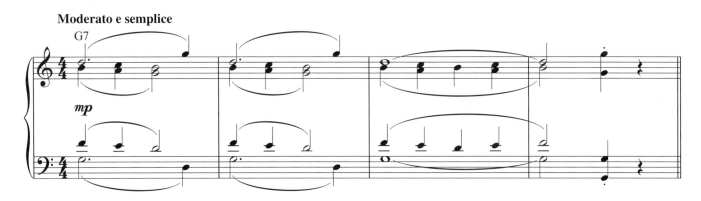

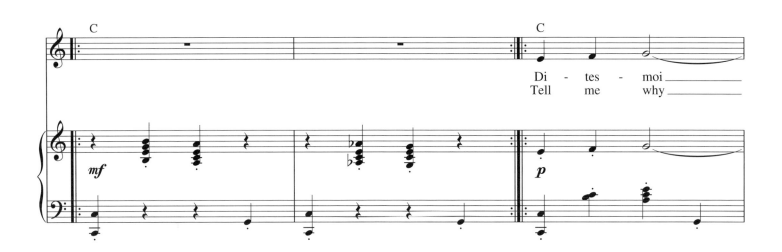

Di - tes - moi _____
Tell me why _____

_____ Pour - quoi _____ La vie est bel - le,
_____ The sky _____ is filled with mu - sic,

DO-RE-MI
from *The Sound of Music*

Lyrics by Oscar Hammerstein II
Music by Richard Rodgers

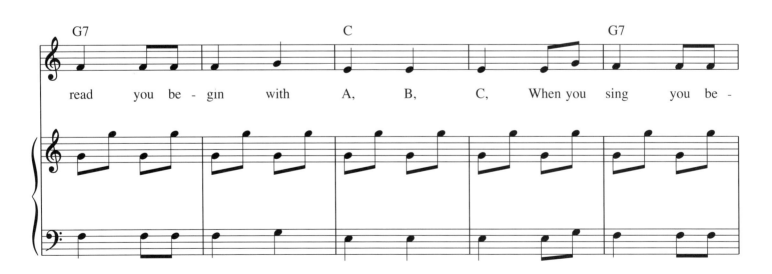

EDELWEISS
from *The Sound of Music*

Lyrics by Oscar Hammerstein II
Music by Richard Rodgers

THE FARMER AND THE COWMAN

from *Oklahoma!*

Lyrics by Oscar Hammerstein II
Music by Richard Rodgers

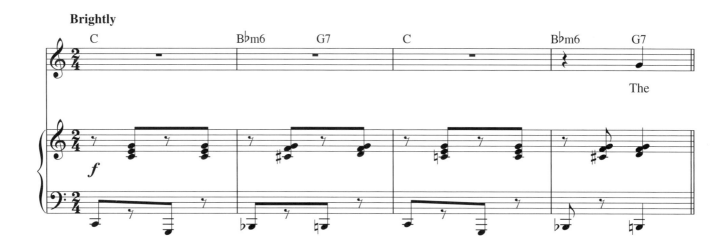

Cow - boys dance with the farm - ers' daugh - ters, farm - ers dance with the

ranch - ers' gals. _____

I'd like to say a word for the
like to teach you all a lit - tle

farm - er: _____ He come out west and made a lot of
say - in', _____ and learn the words by heart the way you

I ENJOY BEING A GIRL
from *Flower Drum Song*

Lyrics by Oscar Hammerstein II
Music by Richard Rodgers

GETTING TO KNOW YOU

from *The King and I*

Lyrics by Oscar Hammerstein II
Music by Richard Rodgers

learn-ing (You'll for-give me if I boast.) And I've now be-come an

ex - pert On the sub-ject I like most, Get-ting to know you.

Refrain (gracefully and not fast)

Get-ting to know you, get-ting to know all a - bout you _____

Get-ting to like you, get-ting to hope you like me _____

26

A HUNDRED MILLION MIRACLES

from *Flower Drum Song*

Lyrics by Oscar Hammerstein II
Music by Richard Rodgers

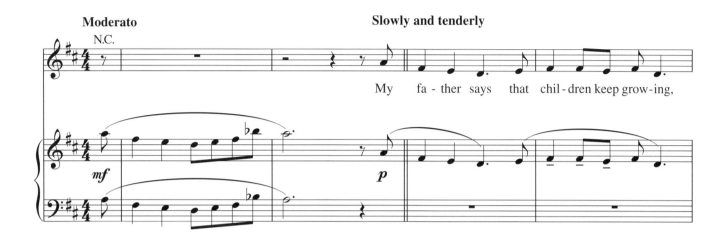

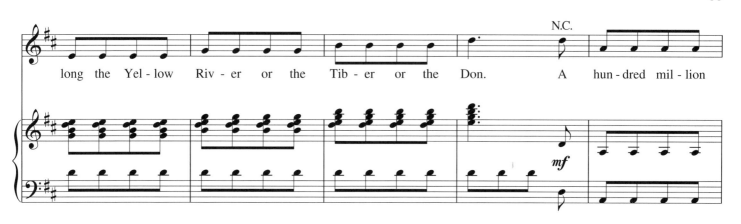

long the Yel - low Riv - er or the Tib - er or the Don. A hun - dred mil - lion

N.C.

mf

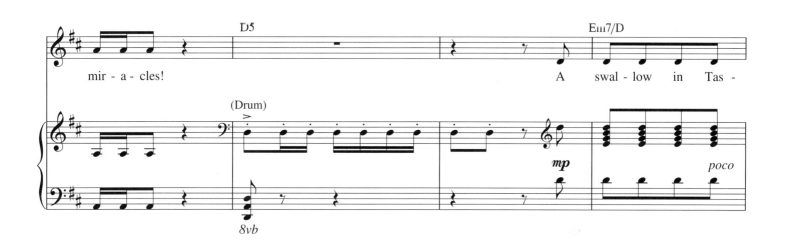

mir - a - cles! A swal - low in Tas -

D5

E♭7/D

(Drum)

mp *poco*

8vb

man - ia is sit - ting on her eggs, And sud - den - ly those eggs have wings and

a poco cresc.

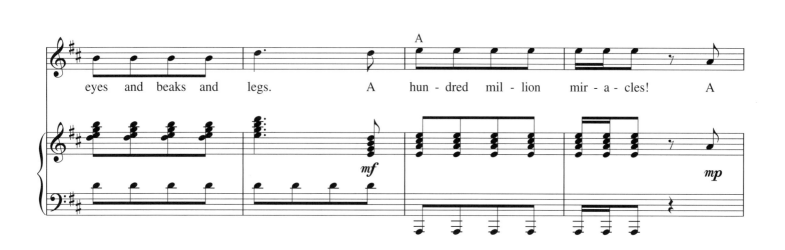

eyes and beaks and legs. A hun - dred mil - lion mir - a - cles! A

A

mf

mp

I WHISTLE A HAPPY TUNE

from *The King and I*

Lyrics by Oscar Hammerstein II
Music by Richard Rodgers

IMPOSSIBLE

from *Cinderella*

Lyrics by Oscar Hammerstein II
Music by Richard Rodgers

IN MY OWN LITTLE CORNER

from *Cinderella*

Lyrics by Oscar Hammerstein II
Music by Richard Rodgers

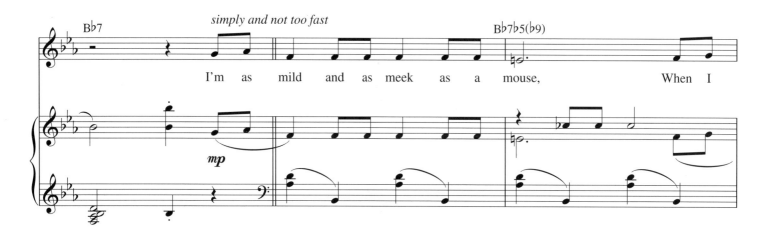

I'm as mild and as meek as a mouse, When I

hear a com-mand I o-bey, But I know of a spot in my

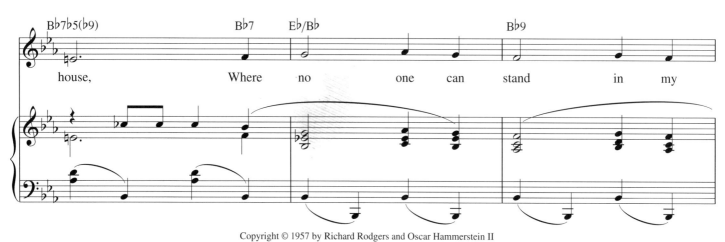

house, Where no one can stand in my

OH, WHAT A BEAUTIFUL MORNIN'

from *Oklahoma!*

Lyrics by Oscar Hammerstein II
Music by Richard Rodgers

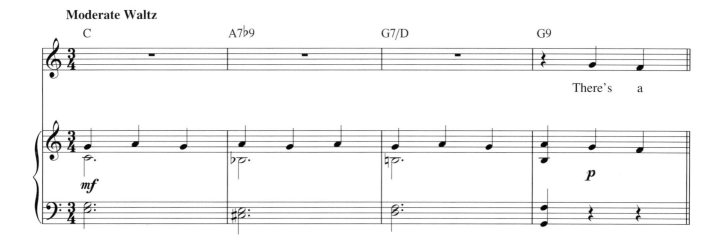

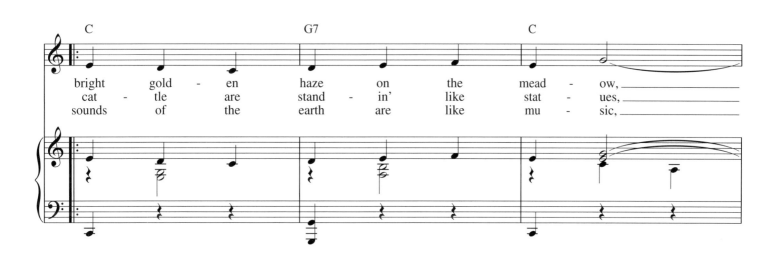

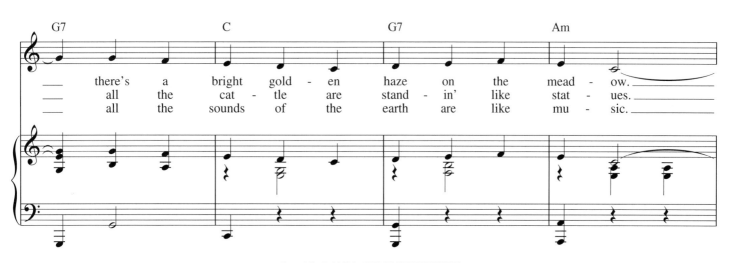

MY FAVORITE THINGS

from *The Sound of Music*

Lyrics by Oscar Hammerstein II
Music by Richard Rodgers

STEPSISTERS' LAMENT

from *Cinderella*

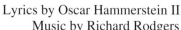

Lyrics by Oscar Hammerstein II
Music by Richard Rodgers

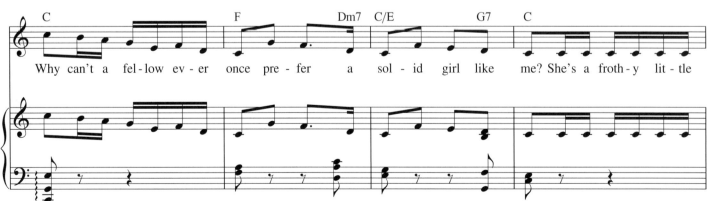

Why would a fel-low want a girl like her, a frail and fluf-fy beau - ty?

Why can't a fel-low ev - er once pre-fer a sol - id girl like me? She's a froth-y lit - tle

TEN MINUTES AGO
from *Cinderella*

Lyrics by Oscar Hammerstein II
Music by Richard Rodgers

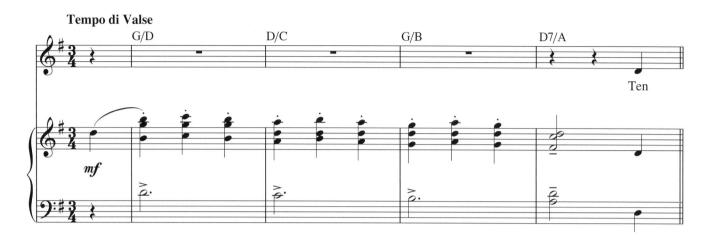

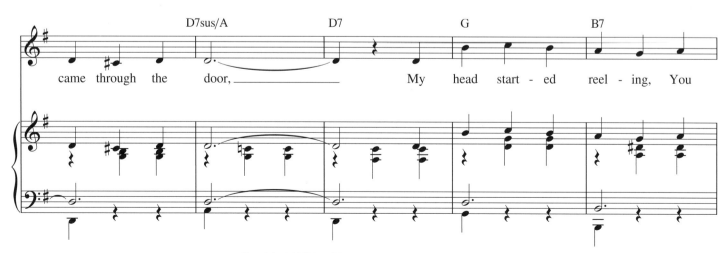

62

ABOUT THE ENHANCED CD

In addition to full performances and piano accompaniments playable on both your CD player and computer, this enhanced CD also includes tempo adjustment software for computer use only. This software, known as Amazing Slow Downer, was originally created for use in pop music to allow singers and players the freedom to independently adjust both tempo and pitch elements. Because we believe there may be valuable educational use for these features in classical and theatre music, we have included this software as a tool for both the teacher and student. For quick and easy installation instructions of this software, please see below.

In recording a piano accompaniment we necessarily must choose one tempo. Our choice of tempo, phrasing, ritardandos, and dynamics is carefully considered. But by the nature of recording, it is only one option.

However, we encourage you to explore your own interpretive ideas, which may differ from our recordings. This new software feature allows you to adjust the tempo up and down without affecting the pitch. We recommend that this tempo adjustment feature be used with care and insight.

The audio quality may be somewhat compromised when played through the Amazing Slow Downer. This compromise in quality will not be a factor in playing the CD audio track on a normal CD player or through another audio computer program.

INSTALLATION INSTRUCTIONS:

For Macintosh OS 8, 9 and X:
• Load the CD-ROM into your CD-ROM Drive on your computer.
• Each computer is set up a little differently. Your computer may automatically open the audio CD portion of this enhanced CD and begin to play it.
• To access the CD-ROM features, double-click on the data portion of the CD-ROM (which will have the Hal Leonard icon in red and be named as the book).
• Double-click on the "Amazing OS 8 (9 or X)" folder.
• Double-click "Amazing Slow Downer"/"Amazing X PA" to run the software from the CD-ROM, or copy this file to your hard disk and run it from there.
• Follow the instructions on-screen to get started. The Amazing Slow Downer should display tempo, pitch and mix bars. Click to select your track and adjust pitch or tempo by sliding the appropriate bar to the left or to the right.

For Windows:
• Load the CD-ROM into your CD-ROM Drive on your computer.
• Each computer is set up a little differently. Your computer may automatically open the audio CD portion of this enhanced CD and begin to play it.
• To access the CD-ROM features, click on My Computer then right click on the Drive that you placed the CD in. Click Open. You should then see a folder named "Amazing Slow Downer". Click to open the "Amazing Slow Downer" folder.
• Double-click "setup.exe" to install the software from the CD-ROM to your hard disk. Follow the on-screen instructions to complete installation.
• Go to "Start," "Programs" and find the "Amazing Slow Downer" folder. Go to that folder and select the "Amazing Slow Downer" software.
• Follow the instructions on-screen to get started. The Amazing Slow Downer should display tempo, pitch and mix bars. Click to select your track and adjust pitch or tempo by sliding the appropriate bar to the left or to the right.
• Note: On Windows NT, 2000, XP, and Vista, the user should be logged in as the "Administrator" to guarantee access to the CD-ROM drive. Please see the help file for further information.

MINIMUM SYSTEM REQUIREMENTS:

For Macintosh:
Power Macintosh; Mac OS 8.5 or higher; 4 MB Application RAM; 8x Multi-Session CD-ROM drive

For Windows:
Pentium, Celeron or equivalent processor; Windows 95, 98, ME, NT, 2000, XP, Vista; 4 MB Application RAM; 8x Multi-Session CD-ROM drive